Light and Shade

Shall we ...

sit with a friend in the cool shade and look at the spring sunshine warming the earth. Touch the soft green leaves and feel how soft they are. Stand under a tree and look at the patterns the leaves make.

Lay a white sheet on the ground to see the light and shadow dance. Make a den with a semi-transparent roof. Sit under a white umbrella on a rainy day to listen and watch the patterns the rain

Create a shadow sheet inside to watch our silhouettes. Dance outside on a spring day and watch our shadows move. Watch as animals scurry across the leaves above our heads.

Spot the holes that bugs have eaten. Create a shadow dance outside on a sunny day. Chase our shadows.

Flowers and buds

Shall we ...

collect some petals and make petal perfume. Put the perfume into some miniature bottles and label them. Design a shelf to put the mixtures on. Talk about being wrapped up cosy and warm. Wrap ourselves up in blankets and read a book. Curl up small and then slowly stretch out. Play hide and seek in the bushes. Make a den and curl up inside. Find a tiny space and hide inside. Collect objects and wrap them up. Go for a walk to see other buds and leaves. Take a photograph of a bud every day to show how it opens. Try to roll up leaves to make them small like a bud.

Spirals

Shall we ...

look at a fern unfurling and explore other spirals. Spin, twist and curl up like a fern. Turn around and spiral in the air. Make a giant spiral of stones.

Create really tiny spirals with grass, seeds or grit. Make a giant spiral so large you can run around it. Make it on the sand, in a field, with ribbon in the yard.

Take the ribbons to the top of the hill and feel the wind spin them around. Twirl and burl around and around and fall over on the grass.

Go for a walk and think of all the words that mean turn. Each time we say one we have to turn and spiral.

Gently start to unfurl a bud to find the soft green hair on the leaf.

Look inside all the new flowers and try to work out if it unfurls or simply opens.

Weaving

Shall we ...

investigate an old nest by taking it apart to look at how the bird wove it all together. Make a nest from twigs. Make a weaving ring from green twigs and thread grasses in and out.

Run in and out of the trees weaving around. Find lots of willow and hazel to play in and change direction every time we touch a tree. Create a giant nest from cushions or logs for us to sit in.

Weave sticks and grasses in and out of the fence. Find a net with smaller holes to make our hands work more efficiently. Find the smallest net to make some tiny weaving.

Make an exciting place for birds to eat with chutes, food trays and little shelters.

Walls

Shall we ...

find small stones to put in row to make a boundary. Look for flat stones to layer up like a dry stone wall. Try to make a cairn with tiny rocks. Make a giant cairn with large rocks that we have to lift together.

Go for a walk and see all the cairns on the hill. Go for a walk to see how important the cairns are to help mountaineers find their way. Make a layered 'mountain' with bands of different rocks.

Collect some strong sticks and put them in the ground to weave willow or hazel in and out of them. Bend soft branches down to make a bender den. Collect some small bricks and stones to make a wall.

Use old bricks to make an enclosure. Go for a walk and look at the walls along the way. Take a camera to photograph close up images of the walls.

Look at the shapes and patterns on the wall. Create a wall around a puddle. Make little fields on the lawn for all the animals to live in.

Mud

Shall we ...

Find as many worm casts as we can. Create mud towers in all different shapes. Make muddy footprints. Look at all the different types of soil, the colour, the texture and the way it sticks together. Make mud pies. Make chocolate milk shake or brown soup. Create mud paint. Use a stick to paint with. Use a leaf to draw on. Use hands to create wonderful patterns. Make some clay by adding a little bit of water to the soil and mixing it well. Construct a mud picture on a leaf...or a stone...or a piece of bark. Take our shoes and socks off and give our toes a gooey mud bath. Look for a flat area of mud to draw a picture with a stick. Make mud walls with just mud and then with grass and mud.

Bark

Shall we ...

listen to the sound of the sap rising as it creaks its way to the top of the tree. Hug a tree.

Feel the bark of all the trees we walk by. Get to know a tree by really looking at the bark, the branches and the new leaves.

Look with a magnifying glass and a torch for bugs living in the cracks. Use our hands, and finger tips to trace over the patterns on the trunk. Smell the bark.

Look for fallen bits of bark and use them to make a transient picture. Dance in the shadow of a tree. Find old bark and put some colour on it.

Make a bracelet of curled bark and earrings to match. Put water on it and look at the changing colours. Climb the tree and feel the bark on our bare feet.

Hide with a friend and peep out from behind a big tree.

Try to put our arms all the way around a tree and squeeze it tight. Close our eyes and feel the bark. Look for different colours and textures of bark.

Feathers

Shall we ...

collect some feathers and tickle with them. Find some binoculars and make a hide to watch the birds. Float a feather on the water. Blow a feather in the air. Balance a feather on your nose.

Dance in feathers and stick some in our hair. Watch a feather float down the stream. Sort the feathers and find the longest one. Look at feathers and try to work out where they come from.

Make a dream catcher from willow, wool and feathers. Take the binoculars out to see what we see. Make a food cone with seeds and fat and take it to the bird table.

Watch the birds and talk about the colours that we see. Watch as the wind ruffles the feathers on the birds at the table. Watch the birds fly on the breeze and use their wing feathers to balance.